To parents and teachers

We hope you and the children will enjoy reading this story in either English or French. The story is simple, but not *simplified* so the language of the French and the English is quite natural but there is lots of repetition.

At the back of the book is a small picture dictionary with the key words and how to pronounce them. There is also a simple pronunciation guide to the whole story on the last page.

Here are a few suggestions on using the book:

• Read the story aloud in English first, to get to know it. Treat it like any other picture book: look at the pictures, talk about the story and the characters and so on.

• Then look at the picture dictionary and say the French names for the key words. Ask the children to repeat them. Concentrate on speaking the words out loud, rather than reading them.

• Go back and read the story again, this time in English *and* French. Don't worry if your pronunciation isn't quite correct. Just have fun trying it out. Check the guide at the back of the book, if necessary, but you'll soon pick up how to say the French words.

• When you think you and the children are ready, you can try reading the story in French only. Ask the children to say it with you. Only ask them to read it if they are keen to try. The spelling could be confusing and put them off.

• Above all encourage the children to have a go and give lots of praise. Little children are usually quite unselfconscious and this is excellent for building up confidence in a foreign language.

Published by b small publishing
The Book Shed, 36 Leyborne Park, Kew, Richmond, Surrey, TW9 3HA, UK
www.bsmall.co.uk
© b small publishing, 2005
1 2 3 4 5
All rights reserved.
Design: *Lone Morton and Louise Millar*   Editorial: *Catherine Bruzzone and Susan Martineau*
Production: *Madeleine Ehm*
Colour reproduction: *Vimnice Printing Press Co. Ltd.* Printed in China by *WKT Co. Ltd.*
ISBN-13: 9781902915166   ISBN-10: 1-902915-16-X (UK French hardback)
British Library Cataloguing in Publication Data. A catalogue record for this book is available from the British Library.

George the goldfish

Georges
le poisson rouge

Lone Morton

Pictures by Leighton Noyes
French by Marie-Thérèse Bougard

b small publishing

Harry has a goldfish.
His name is George.

Harry a un poisson rouge.
Il s'appelle Georges.

George swims round and round his bowl.
Harry loves to watch him.

Georges fait le tour de son aquarium.
Harry adore le regarder.

But one day Harry's goldfish dies.

Mais un jour, le poisson rouge
de Harry meurt.

Harry is very sad and he cries.

Harry est très triste et il pleure.

His mother hugs him.
"George made you happy."

Sa maman lui fait un gros câlin.
"Tu aimais bien Georges, hein?"

"We will bury him in the garden," she says. "And he will make the garden happy."

"On va l'enterrer dans le jardin", dit-elle. "Et il rendra le jardin heureux."

Harry paints a small box.

Harry peint une petite boîte.

He puts George on some leaves
in the box.

Il pose Georges sur des feuilles
dans la boîte.

It's summer.
Harry and his mother dig
a hole under the tree.

C'est l'été.
Harry et sa maman creusent
un trou sous l'arbre.

Harry puts the box in the hole
and covers it with earth.

Harry met la boîte dans le trou
et la recouvre de terre.

His mother plants three flower bulbs.

Sa maman plante trois oignons de fleurs.

"Now George will help the garden to grow. Wait and see," says Harry's mother.

"Maintenant Georges va aider le jardin à pousser. Tu vas voir", dit la maman de Harry.

In the autumn, all the leaves fall from the tree.

Pendant l'automne, toutes les feuilles tombent de l'arbre.

In the winter, it is cold and it snows.

Pendant l'hiver, il fait froid et il neige.

And then, in the spring, three little shoots appear.

Et puis, au printemps, trois petites pousses sortent de terre.

Every day, they grow...
Tous les jours, elles poussent...

and grow...
et poussent...

and grow.
et poussent.

One morning, Harry looks out of the
window and sees three yellow flowers.

Un matin, Harry regarde par la
fenêtre et voit trois fleurs jaunes.

Harry and his mother run out into
the garden.

Harry et sa maman se précipitent
dans le jardin.

"You see, George helped them to grow tall and beautiful," says his mother.

"Tu vois, Georges les a aidées à devenir grandes et belles", dit sa maman.

Harry smiles.

Harry sourit.

Pronouncing French

Don't worry if your pronunciation isn't quite correct.
The important thing is to be willing to try. The pronunciation
guide here will help but it cannot be completely accurate:

- Read the guide as naturally as possible, as if it were British
  English.

- Put stress on the letters in *italics*, e.g. poo-*seh*.

- Don't roll the r at the end of the word, for example in the French
  word **le** (the): ler.

If you can, ask a French person to help and move on as soon as
possible to speaking the words without the guide.

Note French adjectives usually have two forms, one for masculine
and one for feminine nouns, e.g. **grand** and **grande.**

Words Les mots

leh moh

goldfish
le poisson rouge

ler pwah-*soh* roo-jsh

mother
la maman

lah mam-*oh*

tree
l'arbre

larbr'

tall
grand/grande

groh/grond

leaf/leaves
la feuille/les feuilles

lah fer-*yee*/leh fer-*yee*

flower
la fleur

la flurr

garden
le jardin

ler shar-*dah*

beautiful
beau/belle

boh/bel

to grow
pousser

poo-*seh*

happy
heureux/
heureuse

er-*rer*/er-*rerz*

to smile
sourire

soo-*reer*

sad
triste

treest

to cry
pleurer

pler-*reh*

spring
le printemps

ler prah-*toh*

summer
l'été

leh-*teh*

autumn
l'automne

low-*ton*

winter
l'hiver

lee-*vair*

cold
froid/froide

frwah/frwad

it snows
il neige

eel neshj

A simple guide to pronouncing this French story

Georges le poisson rouge
shor-jsh ler pwah-*soh* roo-jsh

Harry a un poisson rouge.
aree ah ahn pwah-*soh* roo-jsh

Il s'appelle Georges.
eel sa*pel* shor-jsh

Georges fait le tour de son aquarium.
shor-jsh feh ler toor der son akwah-ree-*oom*

Harry adore le regarder.
aree a*door* ler rer-gard-*eh*

Mais un jour, le poisson rouge de Harry meurt.
meh ahn shoor ler pwah-*soh* roo-jsh der *aree* murr

Harry est très triste et il pleure.
aree eh treh treest eh eel plurr

Sa maman lui fait un gros câlin.
sah mam-*oh* lwee feh ahn groh ka*lah*

"Tu aimais bien Georges, hein?"
too eh-*meh* bee-*ah* shor-jsh, ahn

"On va l'enterrer dans le jardin", dit-elle.
oh vah lon-tair-*eh* doh ler shar-*dah*, deet-el

"Et il rendra le jardin heureux."
eh eel ron*drah* ler shar-*dah* er-*rer*

Harry peint une petite boîte.
aree pah oon p'*teet* bwat

Il pose Georges sur des feuilles dans la boîte.
eel pohz shor-jsh soor deh fer-*yee* doh lah bwat

C'est l'été.
seh leh-*teh*

Harry et sa maman creusent un trou sous l'arbre.
aree eh sah mam-*oh* krerz ahn troo soo larbr'

Harry met la boîte dans le trou et la recouvre de terre.
aree meh lah bwat doh ler troo eh lah re*koovr'* der tair

Sa maman plante trois oignons de fleurs.
sah mam-*oh* plohnt trwah on-*yoh* der flurr

"Maintenant Georges va aider le jardin à pousser."
man-t'n-*di* shor-jsh vah eh-*deh* ler shar*dah* ah poo-*seh*

"Tu vas voir", dit la maman de Harry.
too vah vvah, dee lah mam-*oh* der *aree*

Pendant l'automne, toutes les feuilles tombent e l'arbre.
pon-*doh* lov-*ton*, toot leh fer-*yee* tomb der larbr'

Pendant l'hiver, il fait froid et il neige.
pon-*doh* ee-*vair*, eel feh frwah eh eel neshj

Et puis, au printemps, trois petites pousses sortent e terre.
eh pwee*oh* prah-*toh*, trwah p'*teet* poos sort der tair

Tous les jours, elles poussent, et poussent, et poussent.
too leh joor, el poos, eh poos, eh poos

Un man, Harry regarde par la fenêtre
ahn m*ah*, *aree* rer-*gard* pah lah f'*netr'*

et voit trois fleurs jaunes.
eh vw* trwah flurr shown

Harry et sa maman se précipitent dans le jardin
aree e*ah* mam-*oh* ser preh-see-*peet* doh ler shar-*dah*

"Tu vis, Georges les a aidées
too v*ih*, shor-jsh leh-zah eh-*deh*

à devnir grandes et belles", dit sa maman.
ah d*neer* grond eh bel, dee sah mam-*oh*

Harry sourit.
aree *s*ree